I never thought KNIX won an award they didn't deserve! Never seen a station compare anywhere---top to bottom!

Buck Owens w/Sandy Lovejoy
Owner—KNIX-FM from 1968-1999

"For me, when I think of the brilliance of Buck Owens as a businessman, I think of radio. Buck loved everything about country airwaves, the way local stations reached communities and promoted music. While other artists threw away their fortunes on foolish endeavors, Buck went with his heart. KNIX, with its red, white, & blue Buckaroo guitar logo, helped define the country music we love. And it continues to influence it to this day. Just like its founding father."

— Brad Paisley
Singer-Songwriter

Buck Owens once said to me; "Dwight, people told me I was crazy and I ain't never gonna make a dime of my money back buying an FM radio station way out in the middle of the desert."

In 1968 Buck had purchased KNIX-FM in Phoenix, Arizona for the bargain price of $75,000 and the naysayers were putting him down. I'm sure he must have had second thoughts on the purchase in those lean early years.

What they didn't realize was that Buck had been in radio before he was a big star as partial owner of a station in Tacoma, Washington in the late 50's and was already a saavy businessman. He had an intuitive understanding of the broadcasting business and its connection to an audience. He had been born into the golden age of radio and loved it as a young man.

Buck had a "Tom Joad-Grape's of Wrath" attitude growing up. The poverty stricken family had migrated from Denton, Texas to Mesa, Arizona during the dust bowl years and he told me that they only had one toothbrush the whole family shared and how that made him ashamed to the point of anger where he vowed; "I ain't never gonna be poor when I grow up."

I met Buck at his original radio station, KUZZ in Bakersfield in late 1987, the same radio and recording studios where songwriter Homer Joy was trying to get him to pay attention to his songwriting and finally did with the song, "Streets of Bakersfield."

I was playing the Kern County fair and wanted to express my admiration and how he had profoundly influenced my music. I never thought we would be friends till the day he died. Buck could be a taskmaster, and he gave you his opinion whether you asked for it or not, usually it was sound advice. Our friendship was unique although we had different personalities. Buck was a driven soul.

I first came to visit KNIX in Phoenix in 1989, the year they debuted their sparkling new state-of-the-art studios. Michael and Buddy Owens met me at the door and gave me the grand tour and always treated me like royalty when I visited. Buck's sons were gentlemen of the first order. I was blown away seeing the station gym. Not many employers offered that perk to their employees at that time.

Buck Owens cared about his circle of people around him. He had an incredible memory and could recall times and dates and everyone who had ever worked for him. He felt he had an obligation to his employee's as well as his music fans. He valued people he could trust, such as his two sons to run the Phoenix radio properties. People were loyal right back to him witness his longtime lawyer, Mr. Schlesinger and manager Jack McFadden both who had worked for him since the sixties. Many of his employees in Bakersfield and Phoenix had been with him 20 plus years.

KNIX became an iconic flagship station that was honored over the years many, many times. The Red, White and Blue guitar and logo became an extension of Buck's personality as a showman and entertainer.

One thing is for certain; "The Odds and Gods smiled down on Buck Owens and his media empire."

Dwight Yoakam
Singer-Songwriter, Host; The Bakersfield Beat on Sirius-XM radio

KNIX

The Buck Owens Years

JIM WEST

Foreword by Michael Owens

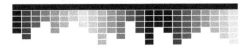

MANY**SEASONS**PRESS

Mesa, Arizona • 2022

FIRST EDITION

KNIX, The Buck Owens Years

Copyright © 2022 by Jim West

Published by Many Seasons Press
(An Imprint of MultimediaPublishingProject.com)
PO Box 50553
Mesa, AZ 85208
480.939.9689 | ManySeasonsPress.com

Cover & book interior designed by Yolie Hernandez
(AZBookDesigner@icloud.com)

ISBN Hardcover: 978-1-7361856-8-1

Library of Congress Control Number: 2022904492

Printed in the United States of America.

Contents

KNIX Timeline

Dedication

LARRY DANIELS — PROGRAMMING GURU,
COUNTRY RADIO HALL OF FAME, NASHVILLE
ARIZONA BROADCASTERS HALL OF FAME INDUCTEE

LARRY DANIELS IS AN AWARD-WINNING radio programming executive. For over 28 years, he contributed greatly to KNIX becoming an iconic and wildly successful radio station. Daniels came to work each day with a laser beam focus and a fire and passion to be a winner. His work ethic was exemplary. Buck Owens even commented; "Larry treated KNIX as if it was his own station."

Daniels compiled weekly music logs by hand and "polled" listeners on what songs they wanted to hear or not hear. Besides sending out surveys to listeners he did "focus" group studies of the music. By the late 1970's computers made that chore easier. Daniels' strategic research and music mix lead to huge ratings.

Larry Daniels had been a part of the local Bakersfield music scene. In the early sixties his group, LARRY "Shotgun" DANIELS

AND THE BUCKSHOTS, performed at many of the same legendary honky tonks that Buck Owens and Merle Haggard had once haunted in that working-class oil and farming boom town in California's San Joaquin Valley.

Larry Daniels was smart, clever and innovative. When recruiting new radio air personalities he would travel around, sit in a motel room then spin the local radio dial, listen and "bank" names of possible future announcers. Over the years he hired, influenced and "mentored" hundreds of broadcasters. He was widely recognized and respected in the country music industry winning many awards in programming including induction into the COUNTRY RADIO HALL OF FAME in Nashville. Mr. Daniels was also inducted into the ABA-ARIZONA BROADCASTERS HALL OF FAME in 2020, an honor that was long overdue.

We proudly DEDICATE this book to our friend Mr. Larry Daniels.

Top: Courtesy of Author

Bottom: Courtesy of WSM Promotions

Foreword

MICHAEL OWENS, VP/GM 1978-1999

Sometime in early 1979—about a year after I became General Manager of KNIX-AM/FM—we were struggling with the ratings and revenue. We were 10th or 12th in the ratings at the time, trying hard to break through and be a player in this big Phoenix market.

We came up with an idea for a promotion and teamed with a local independent gas station (GIANT) to sell gas at 10 cents a gallon. (Gas was selling for about 80 cents per gallon.) We began promoting on air the specific location only an hour before it went on sale—which created total CHAOS. We only had a total of 16-18 people at both stations, so we were short-staffed and ill-prepared. But we received a tremendous amount of television and newspaper coverage.

I knew the promotion was successful when I heard Mike Nolan, traffic reporter for KOY, the no. 1 station in town then and the only station that had a traffic reporter in a plane, directing people away from our promotion site because it was causing a huge traffic jam. I'll never forget he told listeners to stay away because "some stupid radio station and crazy general manager" had come up with a ridiculous promotion!

The next rating period KNIX was No. 1 in the market, the first of many to come and the "beginning of something big."

KNIX became one of the most profitable and well-respected broadcast stations in the nation. It was a challenging, hardworking, fun, exciting place to be. For my part, it was remarkable being there with all the talented people who made it happen.

When Jim told me he was going to write a pictorial book about KNIX I thought well that's nice. When he said it was going to be about the Buck Owens years, I thought great, even better. Then he told me it was going to be dedicated to our longtime friend and Program Director Larry Daniels and I got excited!

I met Larry Daniels when I was 14 and started working for him as a DJ at 16 in Bakersfield, California. I was with Dad when he rehired him as Program Director from Fresno to work for him at KTUF/KNIX in 1971.

Larry had a hard task ahead of him. Both stations weren't successful and losing money each month. The stations went through several managers while Larry struggled to gain ratings.

I was working as GM in Bakersfield at KUZZ for a little over 2 years when I became VP for Buck Owens Broadcasting and began overseeing the Phoenix stations. On one of my monthly trips over, Larry told me he had been offered a job at our competitor, KJJJ. He was tired of the turnover in GM's and thought it might be a good move for him to make. I asked him to wait on making a final decision and that I would move to Phoenix as the GM.

I went back to Bakersfield trying to figure out how I was going to make that happen. I'm 27 years old, going through a divorce with 2 kids at the time. Somehow, I had to convince Dad and my Aunt Dorothy (she was running the day to day operations of Buck Owens Enterprises) to let me leave Bakersfield and move to Phoenix. It took a couple of days of discussions, but they agreed. I'm sure they thought I would go over and come running back in 6 months from this daunting task. I moved over March 1st, 1978 and Larry stayed at the station. Our morning man W. Steven Martin played a HUGE role in talking Larry into staying before I moved over.

I was able to give Larry the tools he needed to improve the music research and programming, hired Bob Podolsky as sales manager, started marketing the station with contests, billboards, TV and had a phenomenon called URBAN COWBOY happening. Two years later KNIX was number 1. All of those things had to happen in that order at precisely that time and they did.

I have terrific memories of the glory days of KNIX in the Buck Owens years. I hope you enjoy seeing and reading the pictorial Jim has put together.

Michael Owens VP/GM

1978-1999

Acknowledgments

*T*HERE ARE COUNTLESS PEOPLE to thank for helping get this project off the ground and into print. I'm blessed that Larry Daniels believed enough to hire me in 1979 giving me the chance to be part of country radio history, although none of us knew what was ahead at the time in the fickle world of radio!

The Owens brothers, Michael and Buddy Alan got excited when we approached them with plans to document, mostly in pictures, the memories we all shared at the station. What stories Michael and Buddy could tell of not only being the sons of a country music legend but to also have a second country legend in Merle Haggard as a step-father when Haggard was married to their mother Bonnie Owens, yet a third Bakersfield music icon! How unique is that?

A huge THANK YOU to many of the talented KNIX alumni that contributed their thoughts and feelings about the station. Thanks to; Vicki Fiorelli-Starkovich, Brian McNeal, Dan Schaffer, "Layback" Lennie Roberts, John Baker, W. Steven Martin, Dick Leighton, Mike Brady, John Michaels, Doug Brannan, Leyla Kirdar-Haupert, Patty Kincaid, Tom Wright, Shanna McCoy, Kathy Meris-Morales, Bob Podolsky, Willie DeLoon, Tim Hattrick, Tom Jennings, Steve Wood, Al Tessitore, Bobby Lewis, Steve Goddard, Steve Harmon, Chris Braden, R.J.Curtis, Keith Ritchie, Mary Morrison, Jeff Munn, Stephan Kaufman and Larry and Marilyn Daniels.

Special thanks go to Michael Owens and Buddy Alan Owens who trusted me to research an accurate compilation of pictures around an historic timeline that KNIX Magazine editor, the late Sandy Lovejoy had researched and written! Sandy is deeply missed.

There were many other past alumni that contributed to KNIX in that era but unfortunately space limitations prevent us from including everyone!

Many listeners also gave us their comments, thoughts and memories. We found many longtime KNIX listeners "teared-up" and became emotional remembering old memories of how much they loved this radio station and how it made a huge impact on their lives. We are grateful for your faithful dedication and love of the station. Listeners drove our success!

Lon Helton with trade magazine COUNTRY AIRCHECK in Nashville also encouraged and contributed as did country stars BRAD PAISLEY and DWIGHT YOAKAM, long time proteges of Buck Owens. Thank you to LeeAnn Enns and Jim Shaw of the Buck Owens Private Foundation for assistance.

Finally, thanks go to Steve Wood, Alan Sledge, Steve Goddard and Beve Cole, who all strongly encouraged me to follow through and not give up, like I almost did, on the idea for the book. Special thanks to my publisher Yolie Hernandez for her dedication in making this book sparkle. I'm grateful. You are a joy to work with.

It was a unique and special time in radio broadcasting that will likely never be duplicated. A lot of great memories were made in those "Buck Owens" ownership years. There seemed to be a little MAGIC in and on the air! You could feel it when you walked in the door! Today, the radio industry has drastically changed. Time does change everything. Michael Owens' leadership and Larry Daniels' programming skills and many talented professionals kept the boat on an even keel through its colorful journey of success. We were all in the right place at the right time and blessed to be along for the ride.

Jim West
August 2020

Introduction

KNIX, THE BUCK OWENS YEARS

Of the 15,000 or so FCC licensed radio stations in the United States there has always been a handful of iconic radio signals that became well known and super served their communities. Many were pioneer stations establishing themselves during the infancy of the radio spectrum. Some great call letters come to mind; WABC, WLS, KOA, KFI, KMOX, WSM, KOB, KOMA, KOY.

Out in the desert southwest there was one station that would grow to become a ratings juggernaut. That station was KNIX-FM in Phoenix, Arizona. The station has quite a storied past. But its popularity with listeners did not happen overnight!

Original owners John and Donna Karshner and their young son signed the station on the air in December of 1961 with only 3100 watts and a beautiful music format. It was obscure and floundered at the bottom of the local radio ratings as not many people owned FM radios then. On weekends the station had instructional programs on how to speak French and German!

The true timeline for the station's success starts with the emergence of a country singer who had migrated west from Sherman, Texas with his family when he was a child. Alvis Edgar Owens Jr, better known as Buck Owens, was 8 years old in 1937 when his struggling family joined the migration of "Okies" and "Texans" escaping the dust bowl that plagued that area during the Great Depression. Their intended destination was the promised land of California. However, a broken trailer hitch had them settling with relatives in Mesa, Arizona, a suburb of Phoenix for several years.

In the 1940's, young Buck began performing in roadhouses and dancehalls in Arizona, even had his own local radio show with a partner. He was not paid because he was paying his DUES!

In 1951, Owens moved to Bakersfield, California and began a musical apprenticeship in various local honky-tonks including the famous BLACKBOARD CAFÉ and watering hole. Soon he would drive over the "grapevine" to work as a studio musician at the CAPITOL recording studios in Hollywood. He played guitar on other singer's recordings. In 1957, Producer Ken Nelson offered him a recording contract and he slowly began dominating the country charts by the sixties.

Young Buck Owens had a 15 minute radio show over KTYL in Mesa in the 1940's...listeners could drive up to the big picture window and see the performers live on the radio. The first drive in radio station (courtesy of Ray Lindstrom)

KNIX *Timeline*

BUCK OWENS EXPERIENCES PHENOMENAL success in country music, selling over one million records a year in the sixties. His career included 25 number one and another 26 top ten HIT records. In 1965, Owens painted his guitar red, white and blue as a statement of his patriotism. 'He invested his money wisely in Bakersfield real estate and local radio station, KUZZ. He forms a music publishing company (Bluebook) with songwriter Harlan Howard and a talent booking agency (OMAC artists). In 1966, he stars in the BUCK OWENS RANCH TV show in syndication nationwide. In 1969, he joins the cast of HEE HAW on CBS. It continues on in syndication nationwide.

Buck and Buckaroo's concert poster, 1967

Top: Buck Owens and lead
guitarist Don Rich on the
Mike Douglas TV show, 1967
(courtesy of Buck Owens
Private Foundation)

Left: Buck Owens and his
Buckaroo's tour bus, 1968
(courtesy of Larry Daniels)

Right: Buck and Don recording at Capitol Records, Hollywood in the 1960's (courtesy of Buck Owens Private Foundation)

Left: Roy Clark and Buck Owens on HEE HAW, 1969 (courtesy of Buck Owens Private Foundation)

1967

Owens buys KYND-AM, Candy-1580, a little "daytimer" station in Tempe, Arizona for $350,000. He changes the call letters to "KTUF." The station starts small with 14 full time and part-time employees in a converted restaurant in Hayden Plaza shopping center before moving to the transmitter building in the nearby Tempe Salt River bottom. Other country competitors in that era were; KHAT, KRDS, KMND, KWBY and KPOK, all daytime stations.

K-TUF Radio "Appreciation Night"

★★★★ STARRING ★★★★

BUCK OWENS & HIS BUCKAROOS

COLISEUM 8 P.M. SAT., AUG. 9th

~~~~ FEATURING ~~~~

★ Ben Colder   ★ Susan Raye

★ The Hagers   ★ Buddy Allen

★ Sheb Wooley

Free Show
DIAL 1580

DIAL K-TUF FOR TICKET INFORMATION

A BUCK OWENS PRODUCTION

Above: Buck Owens provides a free KTUF show to listeners (courtesy of Buck Owens Private Foundation)

Left: KTUF-KNIX KICKER STICKER (courtesy of Larry Daniels)

KTUF/KNIX
KICKER STICKER

KTUF "All American Billboard", 1967 (courtesy of Ray Lindstrom)

ELLER

Buck Owens Broadcasting, Inc.

KTUF

DIAL 1580

GIANT *All American Country Radio* 50,000 watts

1968-1970

*N*O PUN INTENDED BUT OWENS BUYS KNIX-FM 102.5 for a "song" and pays only $75,000 in 1968. After experimenting with a brief progressive rock format, Owens converts the station to Country saying; "Country is the only thing I knew anything about." For years the station operated out of a building next to the 50,000-watt AM transmitter. Employees would travel down a dusty dirt road to the station. Sales and office staff worked out of one big room. Studios were in the transmitter building. It was a humble beginning.

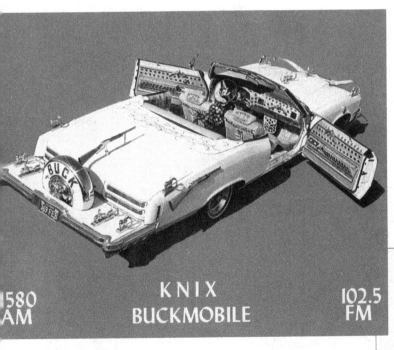

580 AM KNIX BUCKMOBILE 102.5 FM

Left: KNIX "Buckmobile" 1970's-80's promotional vehicle, now hanging over the bar at Buck Owens Crystal Palace restaurant and museum, Bakersfield. Buck won it in a poker game. Tailor Nudie Cohen designed it originally for Elvis Presley

Bottom left: Early bumper sticker, KTUF-KNIX we stamped out 3 letter radio referring to market leader KOY

Below: Miss KTUF Kris Black drives around town showing "Buck's Corvette" that will be given away on the air in 1967 (courtesy of John Dixon)

KTUF/KNIX—We Stamped Out 3 Letter Radio

COMING !!
K-TUF
COUNTRY MUSIC SPECTACULAR

MERLE HAGGARD and The Strangers

❋ **WAYLON JENNINGS**
❋ **JOHNNY WESTERN**
❋ **GLEN CAMPBELL**
❋ **BONNIE OWENS**
❋ **RED FOLEY**

COLISEUM
FRIDAY, JAN. 19, 8:3

Tickets He

K-TUF 1580
KNIX-FM 102.5
PHOENIX

Above: KTUF Country spectacular 1968. This was the night Glen Campbell found out he'd be hosting the GLEN CAMPBELL GOODTIME HOUR TV SHOW (courtesy of Johnny Western)

Top Right: KTUF-KNIX ambassador, Kris Black, at Easter Egg hunt with the children at LEGEND CITY amusement park, 1971

Bottom right: KTUF-KNIX Easter Egg Hunt at LEGEND CITY amusement park, 1971

Above: KTUF-KNIX Easter Egg Hunt and Buck Owens in concert at LEGEND CITY amusement park, 1971

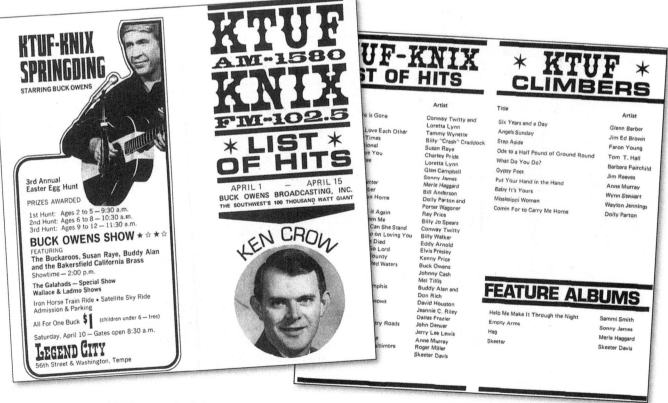

KTUF-KNIX April 1971 music playlist

1971-1972

OWENS HIRES LARRY DANIELS to program both stations which had been' struggling to find an audience. Daniels remembers thinking; "Our only hope is the FM." While AM radio was "King," auto manufacturers were just beginning to install FM radios in new cars. FM offered a clearer static free signal superior to AM. Ratings; KTUF with a 2.2 share and KNIX-FM, a 1.9 share of the market.

Early sixties portrait of a young Larry Daniels (courtesy of Michael Owens)

"We had the honor of being able to hire and work with many talented, creative and listener-friendly people at KNIX. Michael Owens, our general manager had a plan that was always asking; "How do you think our listeners would feel about that." We placed our listeners as a top priority. We established a great research department in our strategies. Through the years, KNIX hosted an incredible number of unique events, like the DOLLY PARTON look-a-like contest where we packed the Mr. Lucky's nightclub with 1000 listeners and 30 Dolly look-a-likes. It was a fun night. We got local TV coverage and front-page pictures in the newspaper, and this was in 1979 when we were still struggling to gain listeners and big ratings. It was gratifying that the Nashville country music industry considered KNIX to be one of the greatest country radio stations in the history of the format."

Larry Daniels, General Program Manager (1971-1999)

"I was doing the morning show in 1973. Buck Owens was in town and when I got off the air one day I was invited to meet with Buck in Larry Daniels office. Buck then said; "Tommy I want to donate KNIX to ASU (Arizona State University), before I do Larry asked me to get your opinion?" I said; "Buck, donating KNIX to ASU would be a huge mistake. I suggested donating the daytime AM station (KTUF) instead. FM stations had not caught on quite yet with listeners but would very soon. Thankfully, Buck decided NOT to donate KNIX-FM to ASU. The KNIX legacy was assured!"

Tom Wright, KNIX mornings (1972-1973)

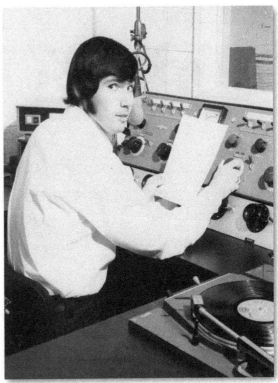

Left: KTUF-KNIX Grand Ole Opry promotion, 1971 (courtesy of Larry Daniels).

Above: Tommy Wright, KTUF-KNIX morning personality, 1972-73 (courtesy of Larry Daniels).

Below: Mike Scott, KTUF-KNIX afternoon personality, 1972-73 (courtesy of Larry Daniels)

1973-1975

*K*TUF-AM CHANGES CALLS TO KNIX-AM and continues to simulcast with the FM. In 1974, Larry Daniels begins to survey listeners by mail, licking stamps and tabulating results by hand; "To keep on track with the music."

Left: Bobby Butler, air personality, 1972 (courtesy of Larry Daniels)

Bottom: Lenny Roberts, singer Zella Lehr, RCA records rep Carson Schreiber with Larry Daniels, 1977, (courtesy of Larry Daniels)

Top: Standing top L to R; Lennie Roberts, W. Steven Martin, Susan Raye, Buck Owens, Bobby Butler, (unknown) Vic Mariani and Larry Daniels, Below; Robin Lee Grube, Singer David Frizzell, Elliot Klein, engineer, Buddy Alan Owens kneeling. Buck, Susan, David and Buddy Alan in town for a listener showcase show, 1973 (courtesy of Len Roberts)

Right: Olivia Newton-John visits the station, 1974. Top L to R: Charlie Ochs, Lennie Roberts, Larry Daniels, ONJ and J.D. Freeman (courtesy of Len Roberts)

1976-1978

*T*HE STATION CONTINUES TO STRUGGLE IN THE RATINGS and see's turnover in General Managers and some air talent. Owens' son, Michael, joins KNIX as VP and GM in 1978. He immediately determines the station has a problem related to a perceived "hayseed" image country music had at the time. Sophisticated advertising clients were not too interested in buying time on the station. However, Daniels research was showing a responsive, quality audience developing as a result of his programming.

The station bolstered audience research methodology that measured listenership and constantly refined the programming. News department was beefed up with several reporters, air personalities started getting out into the public promoting the station and new budgets were set. The first TV spots went on the air in 1979. (Ratings for Spring 1978 was KNIX-AM and KNIX -FM at a 1.3 and 4.1 respectively)

Left: Brian McNeal and singer Johnny Western, 1978 (courtesy of Brian McNeal)

Opposite page from top to bottom: Brian McNeal and singer Jerry Wallace, 1978 (courtesy of Brian McNeal)

Brian McNeal, air personality in production room, 1977 (courtesy of Brian McNeal)

KNIX Gong Show at Mr. Lucky's club, L to R: Robin Grube, Brian McNeal, and on stage Mike Brady and contestant, 1978 (courtesy of Brian McNeal)

"I started on the air in 1973. Back then the station was at the bottom of the ratings heap of 36 stations only to vault to number one by 1980 and stayed there for years. Credit goes to Larry Daniels and Michael Owens. Larry hired announcers who sounded real. We were out meeting the public at charity events, remote broadcasts, concerts and nightclub appearances up to 7 days a week! Everywhere we went the listeners followed. We had a loyal audience. We also embraced the URBAN COWBOY movement that swept the country. It was a great time to be part of the station."

Brian McNeal, Air Talent (1973-1980)

"Larry Daniels hired me in 1977. I was planning on getting out of radio after KHOS, Tucson. He asked me to interview for the job that led to a 45 year career in broadcasting. We did so many events. I remember learning to ice skate in three days before "Layback Lennie Roberts" and I raced each other in an ICE CAPADES promotion with Elmo and Cookie Monster! Two most influential people in my radio career have to be Larry Daniels and Michael Owens."

Mike Brady, On air talent (1977-1980)

1979

Free Beer!
Free Concert!
Free Admission!
When You
"Show Us Your
Country!"

Wednesday, March 24th, at 7 p.m., join KNIX at Graham Central Station, on 33rd Avenue and Indian School. When you get to the door, show us anything that has KNIX on it — hats, mugs, t-shirts, belt buckles, or a KNIX Button — and you'll get in free.

But that's just the beginning. From 7 to 9 p.m., we'll have free beer. And at 10 p.m., enjoy a full concert show by country music star Buck Owens.

You could win cash, too. Because we'll be asking people to "Show us your Country!" and if you do, you'll win cash from KNIX.

Don't miss KNIX's Show us your Country night at Graham Central Station. Free beer. A free concert by Buck Owens. And free admission. All you have to do is "Show us your Country!"

KNIX
ARIZONA COUNTRY
FM STEREO 102 • AM 1580

THE STATION PARTNERED WITH GIANT GAS stations to offer listeners 10 cent a gallon gas in March 1979 at a station on Central Avenue near Camelback Road. At the time, people were complaining that gas prices were getting too high! (Gas was about 80 cents a gallon then.) The promotion caused a huge traffic jam. KOY traffic reporter Mike Nolan told his listeners to avoid the area. The station did get front page newspaper coverage and TV exposure for the stunt.

Above: "Show Us Your Country" promotion with Buck Owens concert at Graham Central Station nightclub.

Right: KNIX 10 cent gas promotion caused a 3 mile traffic jam, 1979.

"Larry Daniels first interviewed me in 1977. A hiring freeze prevented my start until 1979. I'm very grateful Larry remembered me. The job changed my life and elevated my career and the careers of all who worked there. It was the most cohesive and creative place I've ever been. Hundreds of great memories. Like KNIX winning the hideous "traveling trophy" in the Phoenix Jaycee's Rodeo "Calf dressing media event." That ugly ole beat up trophy sat in the station lobby for all to see, or snicker at.

"Dolly Parton once gave me hell (joking around) for coming into her concert late in front of the entire audience. It got a lot of laughs. Then at Willie Nelson's 50th Birthday party the radio staff and Waylon Jennings sang Happy Birthday to him. Willie turned around, looked me square in the eye and said next time "sing it in key." He was yanking my chain too!"

"It was always a pleasure to work for a station who really knew how to Super-serve an audience with the right music mix and personality."

Jim West, Air Talent (1979-1987)

Top: Brian McNeal and Jim West, "shack out back studios," 1979 (courtesy of Sam Schoppenhorst)

Right: Jim West, George Strait and morning personality W. Steven Martin, early 80's (courtesy of WSM Promotions)

KNIX business offices and studios, 1970's-1980's (courtesy of Larry Daniels)

"I arrived at KTUF-KNIX in sales in 1977. The entire staff was housed in a studio and offices and that big 50,000-watt transmitter humming nearby. It was so powerful we joked we could hear the station through our tooth fillings.

"Michael Owens arrived in 1978 as GM. I stayed and became sales manager. From that day forward everything evolved quickly. Michael was magic. We worked smart with marketing and research, TV spots, putting us on a pathway to number one ratings. The research armed us with info to debunk the country "hick" stereotype to advertisers. Michael had the talent and foresight to steer the ship expertly and create the synergy. It was quite a ride!"

Bob Podolsky, Sales Manager (1977-1999)

1980-1982

*S*UCCESS! KNIX SPRING RATINGS REPORTED THE STATION NUMBER ONE with a 9.2 share of total listenership (12 plus). The station begins an incredible run of number one ratings for the stations' target demographic, 25-54 years of age for the next 10 CONSECUTIVE YEARS, except for one rating period. In 1980, the FCC grants KNIX-AM approval to broadcast 24 hours a day in stereo. One of the first AM STEREO stations in the country. A new 5 tower array and transmitter site are built in nearby Mesa.

"I remember the great camaraderie of the AM & FM staffs in the eighties. We were promotionally active at several of the "bazillion" country night spots in the valley. We reached out to as many listeners as we could. Invariably every member of the air staff showed up to support whatever personality was there to do contests and give away prizes that night. We were a cohesive bunch for sure! Michael Owens and Larry Daniels were leaders. What a great place to work."

Dan Schaffer, Air Talent (1980-1987)

Larry Daniels and Michael Owens celebrate the first number one ratings book, 1980, (courtesy of Michael Owens)

"I was straight out of high school in 1979 when I walked into KNIX in September. I was 18 years old, fresh off the farm and scared to death but knew I wanted to be a part of KNIX. Larry Daniels introduced me to Buck Owens. In a loud commanding voice he said; "Welcome to KNIX young man" It was the start of an amazing experience at the greatest radio station in the country! It was common to see major country stars walk the hallways. I was so young I didn't appreciate it until later. I wish I could go back to those days and what it means to so many of us. It was a privilege to be a part of something that will never happen again. I'm grateful to Larry Daniels and Michael Owens to enjoy the KNIX experience."

Steve Wood, Air Talent, Production (1979-1985)

Top: Late singer Eddie Rabbitt, young fan and Dan Schaffer, Mesa, AZ, 1980 (courtesy of Larry Daniels)

Above: Steve Wood hangs out with Glen Campbell, early 80's (courtesy of Steve Wood)

Right: Steve Wood on the air, 1980 (courtesy of Elliot Klein)

In the Summer of 1980 I had the good fortune to join the W. Steven Martin morning show as the pilot flying traffic watch. As a result, this partnership turned into a truly great friendship that has become even stronger today. W made me look good and sound good during those many years on the radio. They were some of the best years of my life.

Dick Leighton, KNIX Traffic watch (1980-1996)

Top left: Traffic Watch reporter Dick Leighton and W. Steven Martin discuss the gossip or news of the day (courtesy of WSM promotions)

Top right: KNIX Traffic Billboards, 1980's (courtesy of the author)

Above: Talented writer and editor for the KNIX magazine, Sandy Lovejoy. Sandy knew all the country stars from Nashville (courtesy of Joel Samuel)

Bottom right: Dick Leighton, KNIX Traffic watch pilot (courtesy of Larry Daniels)

In the early 60's I was a young boy with dreams of somehow making a difference in people's lives by doing something that would make my mother and me proud!

Our family would listen to our radio 24/7. The radio was all we had for entertainment. As I listened I would think about how POWERFUL VOICES were and how WONDERFUL MUSIC sounded from that little box in our kitchen. The voices had such a mystery to them.

My RECORD LIFE started when I would ride my bicycle down a dirt road in Tempe and cut a field of weeds by hand for a bicycle handlebar full of free records. I would take them home and play them at a pretend radio station (KING) that I built in our little laundry room shack and carport. (A home studio, that's never going to happen!)

Every few weeks I would ride to work and then fill my handlebars with all the records I could force on them, most of the records were junk. The next time I worked I thought of a way to improve my chances of getting a few more hit records so I went out and bought "butterfly handlebars' that way I could get more records each time. At that time the little building on Gilbert Drive was called KYND-1580 AM with a 50,000 watt transmitter in the back where an enclosed patio used to stand. The hum from the unit would shake the building when it was on high power. Later the station became K-TUF AM and then KTUF/KNIX AM & FM.

Johnny Cash at the AZ State Fair, L to R: Jim West, then wife Patty, Sheila Roberts, Johnny Cash, contest winners and Len Roberts

W. Steven Martin spent over 25 years at KNIX (courtesy of WSM promotions)

While I was weed whacking outside I was allowed into the little building to cool off, use the bathroom and could watch the DJ through the big glass window, as I watched I thought to myself someday that will be me in there, I HOPE!

Larry Daniels (Program Director) Larry knew the difference between a disc jockey and a radio personality from his band days. Everyone knew if a person was a lead singer or a back-up singer, most of all the people in nightclubs and people listening to the radio audience also knew.

When Larry hired me he told me "JUST BE YOU, HAVE FUN, PEOPLE WILL LOVE YOU" we will leave you alone and did for over 20 years. As I left his office he said by the way "W" you don't need to cut weeds anymore!

Over the years when Larry Daniels was in charge he let me alone and let me create what I called "Theater of the mind" on the air and my show ratings had nowhere to go but UP, in my mind that was why the guitar was pointed UP for twenty years, we were growing in popularity and ratings and people liked what they heard!

Two of the best additions Larry made to my show were the addition of DICK LEIGHTON with traffic watch (still one of my best friends) and SANDY LOVEJOY with artist Features, both of them gave me an edge in my overall ratings.

The largest show dial-in was on Friday at 7:20 a.m. That's when I did my "SHOWER SONG" (soundtrack by Charlie McCoy's ORANGE BLOSSOM SPECIAL) Even if you didn't like country music people would TUNE-in to hear crazy "W" take a shower (yelling and screaming) The ratings would almost double reaching an incredible 25.4 share of people listening to "W" in the morning. One out of four people that lived in metro Phoenix were (as the jingle said) DOIN' IT WITH "W" on the radio. I would always follow the shower song with a cross over country/pop song to keep them to listen even longer.

Over my "GUITAR YEARS" I lived my dreams thanks to people like Larry, listeners and others, my shows ratings, events, remotes, community service projects and ideas made a difference in my popularity, broadcasting careers and a lot of people's lives for over 25 years. The evidence of my work was reflected in every award we received until I left in 1999 and the red, white and blue guitar was put away.

The CMA (Country Music Association) honored me 7 times with TOP FIVE finalist nominations and TWO (CRYSTAL AWARDS) WINS as the TOP RADIO PERSONALITY OF THE YEAR in 1992 and 1999. Proudly I was also inducted into the Country Radio Broadcasters (CRB) HALL OF FAME in Nashville. The CMA FOUNDATION along with Arizona Governor Rose Mofford presented me with one of a very few CMA FOUNDATION AWARDS for outstanding community service for creating my own non-profit 501 (c)-(3) Foundation. Over the past 35 years my 911 Police and Fire Toy Drive has given away over SIX MILLION GIFTS to children in Arizona THROUGH THE HANDS OF A POLICE OFFICER OR FIRE FIGHTER.

In my record life broadcasting years I was proud to have met, interviewed or introduced hundreds of recording artists and in some way helped them along their road to fame but my BIGGEST reward was the people that listened each morning for years that gave me a reason to go to work and do my best every day!

I hope my work, passion and creative way of communication made a difference in their lives during that special time we had together!

I know now my family, friends and most of all my mother is proud of what a little skinny boy from Nebraska did in his record life!

W. Steven Martin, Morning Personality (1973-1999)

Janice was just one of thousands of dedicated KNIX listeners (courtesy of JL Vallee)

The KNIX morning show woke me up to uncontrollable laughter with W. Steven Martin. After that, we listened to Jim West and the rest of the crew all day long. Best days of my life was KNIX radio with all the live concerts and venues. Those were fun times. I'll never forget when I was a little girl dancing on my dad's toes to Buck Owens "Tiger by the Tail."

Janice Lefebvre, Longtime KNIX Listener

Top left: Jim West on the air KNIX-FM, 1981. Top Right: Erik Foxx on KNIX-FM in the eighties (courtesy of Larry Daniels) Above: The Buck Owens KNIX Red, White and Blue guitar was seen everywhere in Arizona (courtesy of WSM Promotions)

1983-1985

*T*HE STATION CONTINUES TO INVEST in its own future and growth. Management smartly plans out strategies for ratings growth and dominance. Air personalities are out in the public eye at major nightclubs featuring country music. New studios are added on to the existing business offices with plans to expand even more in the future.

The "Sticker-On" bumper sticker campaign begins partnering with Circle K food stores to offer listeners up to a $1000 cash if they have a sticker on their car. The contest was a huge success. In the eighties KNIX continues to install state-of-the-art broadcast equipment to better our signal. Every area of operations is scrutinized and upgraded. It paid off in dividends with continued number one ratings.

Above: Young lady modeling KNIX T-shirts (courtesy of Larry Daniels). Left: Sticker on Billboard promotion

Opposite page: KNIX Sticker-on contest promotion, 1980's (courtesy of Stephan Kaufman) and "Layback" Lennie Roberts, afternoons in the 70's and 80's (courtesy of Larry Daniels)

Sticker on. And win cash. KNIX

KNIX
FM STEREO 102 • AM 1580

In 1982 I was working as a weekend jock on KJJJ radio. Steve Wood told me of an opening at KNIX in which I applied. Larry Daniels hired me over the phone and I began working the very next weekend as the station was sending the entire staff to a retreat out of town. I was impressed with the professionalism at KNIX. In my 4 years I was involved in many events. I worked with some incredibly talented radio people at KNIX and I cherish those memories.

Tom (Mihalchick) Jennings, Weekends / part-time (1982-1986)

L to R: L.J. Waggoner, Larry Daniels, Joe Bravo, EPIC records, Ricky Skaggs and Jim West, 1981

Bottom: Dolly Parton and the KNIX Crew with RCA records, Country Radio Seminar, Nashville, 1980's (courtesy of Larry Daniels)

I joined KNIX in 1980 and fortunately built my media career with Owens Broadcasting. We thrived in an environment where everyone believed in a culture of high performance, teamwork and strong leadership. KNIX delivered best in class entertainment experiences to our listeners, community and advertising partners. KNIX produced some of the most memorable concert and promotional events in Arizona. Many still talked about over 30 years later. I'm grateful for lifelong friendships, shared laughter, tears, lots of country dancing and the most amazing memories.

Leyla Kirdar Haupert, Sales
(1980-2014)

Top: Larry Daniels, W. Steven Martin, George Strait, Sandy Lovejoy, Jim West and Doug Brannon, 1985 (courtesy of Chris Braden)

Bottom: KNIX staff celebrate Willie Nelson's 50th birthday at coliseum, 1983, with Waylon Jennings (courtesy of Gary O'Brien)

A memory of working at KNIX is that in 1981 the AM studio was still in the little transmitter building behind the main business office. I was doing the night shift from 7-midnight when a scorpion crawled across the top of the audio console and scared the heck out of me! Another night, a frog hopped over my foot on the floor. Lots of wildlife came out at night in that little studio/transmitter shack. Thankfully a new studio was being built.

Kathy Meris-Morales, Air Talent (1980-1982)

Above: Kathy Meris-Morales, KNIX-AM early 80's (courtesy of Kathy Meris-Morales)

Left: John Michaels, Brian Kelly, Crystal Gayle, Jim West & Doug Brannon, 1986 (courtesy of Doug Brannon)

I have a few great memories of my KNIX days. Actor Mark Harmon (NCIS) was chosen as the "Sexiest Man Alive" by People Magazine in 1986. He was in town and I was interviewing him on the air. While chatting with Harmon I noticed that all of the female station employees had invaded the studio window and were pressing their face against the glass and "staring" at Harmon. As he exited the studio he had to navigate past each woman who threw down their wedding rings in front of him! It was a KODAK moment.

Stephan Kaufman, News Director (1980's)

Top left: KNIX news billboard, 1980's

Above: KNIX Newsroom, 1980's Stephan Kaufman, News Director (courtesy of Larry Daniels)

Left: Stephan Kaufman, Jeff Munn and Larry Clark, KNIX news, 1980's (courtesy of Larry Daniels)

The story of KNIX and Buck Owens is one of the great stories in broadcasting. The dedication to excellence was evident in everything Buck, Michael Owens and Larry Daniels did, along with countless others. The standards they set should and will stand as an example to other broadcasters for years to come. I was honored to play a small part in the story of KNIX, and the lessons I learned there I still use today.

Jeff Munn, KNIX News dept (1981-1988)

Top to bottom: Jeff Munn, KNIX Newsman, Arizona State Capitol, 1980's (courtesy of Larry Daniels)

KNIX News Cruisers, 1980's (courtesy of Chris Braden, Larry Daniels)

KNIX radio staff, Jeff Dayton wins the Mr. Lucky's Wrangler Country Showdown, 1985

1985-1987

SINGER GEORGE STRAIT WAS THE FIRST COUNTRY STAR to do a series of television commercials for KNIX. Other celebrities followed. In April 1987, KNIX is named Country Station of the Year by the Academy of Country Music. The CMA awards follows suit in the fall with KNIX winning top station. No other country station had ever won both an ACM and CMA award in the same year. TUNE-IN Magazine debuts in October, 1987. KNIX-FM is number one again with a 15.3 share 12 plus audience and KNIX-AM with a 2.1 share.

Top: KNIX –FM Studio's late 1980's (courtesy of Larry Daniels)

Bottom: KNIX Charity Basketball team "Droopy Dribblers" would travel the state playing high school teams to raise money for local causes. We mostly lost!

Left: Michael Owens celebrates the ribbon cutting of the KNIX employee gym, 1985 (courtesy of Michael Owens)

Bottom left: KNIX gym trainer Norman Smith with station goodies as incentives to work out at the gym. (courtesy of Larry Daniels)

Bottom right: Norman Smith, KNIX Gym Trainer, 1980's (courtesy of Larry Daniels)

Top: KNIX Gym, Jim West and Charlie Daniels hit the bikes...! (courtesy of Chris Braden)

Above: KNIX Gym, Jim West, Larry Daniels, RCA records rep Carson Schreiber, Ronnie Milsap, Michael Owens, 1985 (courtesy of Chris Braden)

Working at KNIX had been a goal of mine when attending Phoenix College in the 70's and served as an announcer on the campus station KMCR-FM. I learned you had to pay your "dues" to become good enough to work at a radio station in a large market like Phoenix. I spent 6 years perfecting my broadcasting skills at stations in Parker, Yuma and Tucson, Arizona when I was presented the opportunity to work at KNIX.

I started in 1982 as a fill-in announcer then moved to 9-12 noon on the AM side and assigned music director. By 86, I was Promotions and Marketing Director. We were involved in campaigns to win multiple Station of the Year awards. In 1989, I became program manager for the REAL COUNTRY satellite network that Buck Owens Broadcasting had partnered with.

Doug Brannan, KNIX (1982-1990)

1988

ONCE AGAIN, BOTH THE ACM AND CMA HONOR KNIX with Country station of the year trophies. There are now 70 employees housed in 12,000 square feet of office, production and studio space as well as the employee gym that includes a personal trainer on staff, sauna, showers and locker rooms. The company is again, one of the FIRST in Phoenix to offer this perk to employees as an incentive to stay healthy.

> "Buck Owens employed a special group of people who welcomed me, a 14 year old girl, in a wheelchair into their family. I can only hope they know how much it meant to me as well as my parents. Listening to KNIX was so much more than listening to good country music, it was time spent with dear friends, many of whom I am still in touch with today."

Tracey McDaniel, long time dedicated listener

Promotional Billboard "Stand UP for your Country, Say KNIX", 1980's

Top left: KNIX was constantly upgrading broadcast equipment. Ad for audio processor, 1980's (courtesy of Larry Daniels)

Top right: Prior to the internet KNIX published a monthly newsletter, 1980's

Left: Graham Central Station, "Best Little Whorehouse in Texas" promotion, L to R: Jim West, Steve Wood, Leyla Kirdar-Haupert, Dawn Saxton, Larry Daniels and Don Cristi, 1980's

I was fortunate to enjoy 17 years working at KNIX because of Larry Daniels. Started as a weekend jock, then evenings for 9 months and then on to production manager. Larry was such a great coach, boss and friend. His guidance of staff was the reason KNIX dominated Phoenix radio for so long. Buck and Michael Owens created the right environment of facility (one of the best in the nation), mindset of professionalism and encouraging greatness.

Al Tessitore, On-air and Production Manager (1982-1999)

Top left: Al Tessitore, KNIX Production Manager (courtesy of Larry Daniels). Top right: Crazy Wickenburg Inn Christmas party 1984, Bob Podolsky and Michael Owens compete in tricycle races! (courtesy of Chris Braden). Bottom left: KNIX staff outside business offices in the late 1980's (courtesy of Chris Braden). Bottom right: Ruth Calabro was our long time KNIX receptionist and with the station for over 25 years (courtesy of Larry and Marilyn Daniels)

1989

$\mathcal{A}$ NEW 25,000 SQUARE FOOT TWO STORY BUILDING OPENS. In April, KNIX stages "Country Jam 89," two days of live music by Alabama, Waylon Jennings, Willie Nelson and others. Over 150,000 attend. The station partners with Satellite Music Network to broadcast a traditional country format nationwide called REAL COUNTRY. KNIX-AM becomes KCW-AM and is the flagship station serving an eventual 100 nationwide affiliates. KNIX debuts COUNTRY SPIRIT magazine in October produced within the station. Over 75,000 are printed monthly. Sandy Lovejoy is the magazine editor.

The National Association of Broadcasters introduces the annual MARCONI AWARDS to recognize radio stations nationwide for quality and performance! KNIX wins 2, one for overall excellence and one in the country music category. In late 1989, the ratings show KNIX as the DOMINANT station for the ENTIRE DECADE of the 1980s.

KNIX New business office and studio on Gilbert Drive, 1989 (courtesy of Vicki Fiorelli-Starkovich)

My years at KNIX were some of the best of my professional and personal life. The friends and memories will always be with me, reminding me how wonderful it was to work there. From my radio mentor Larry Daniels, Michael and Buddy Owens and all others I worked with, the sense of family will be what I remember most. It truly was a special place and a special time.

George King, KNIX (1985-2003)

Two views of the plush lobby of KNIX studios, 1989 (courtesy of Michael Owens)

One of the biggest things I hold the proudest is that KNIX was always there for our community. KNIX employees are a family, family takes care of family. Many KNIX employees volunteered to help our community in so many ways. The Owens family made a commitment to be of service to our listeners and clients. KNIX still does that today.

Vicki Fiorelli-Starkovich, Marketing and Promotions Manager (1991-1999)

Top: CountryJam 89 concert was a HUGE success. Over 100,000 attended (courtesy of Larry Daniels)

Bottom: Late Production manager Geoff Erb teaching a young man about an audio console (courtesy of Larry Daniels)

Growing up in a very rural place in the 80's and 90's the radio was easily our lifeline to the outside world. W. Steven Martin, Jim West, Steve Wood, R.J.Curtis and my personal idol John Michaels were like friends that always knew exactly what to say, and more importantly play our favorite music. The yearly ARIZONA COUNTRY 500 country song countdown was practically a holiday at our house! The fact the station was owned by the great Buck Owens was icing on the cake. I will always look back at fun memories of KNIX radio being our sole entertainment with great fondness. We were BIG fans.

Jessica Hastings-Solper, dedicated listener from Wittman, Arizona

KNIX was EVERYWHERE with promotional hot and cold air balloons, Rawhide, 1980's (courtesy of Chris Braden)

Thunderbird Balloon classic Balloon meet, 1990's (courtesy of Chris Braden)

1990

COUNTRY SPIRIT MAGAZINE EXPANDS its computer system and begins functioning as an in-house agency for all creative services and a production hub for all print services at the station.

Left: KNIX Country Spirit Magazine with Randy Travis & Roy Rogers (courtesy of Chris Braden)

Below: George King, George Strait and Larry Daniels by George, 1990's (courtesy of Chris Braden)

Top left: Buddy Alan Owens and Larry
Daniels pondering a staff meeting
(courtesy of Michael Owens)

Top right: Larry Daniels with a worried look?
Can't be the ratings?? (courtesy of Larry
Daniels)

Right: Autographed Buck Owens publicity
photo, late 80's (courtesy of Jl Vallee)

1991

KNIX SETS UP A REMOTE BROADCAST FOR A DOWNTOWN PHOENIX PARADE to honor and welcome home military personnel from DESERT STORM! In September, the TV show STEPPIN' OUT debuts with local NBC affiliate Channel 12. Air Personality John Michaels becomes the host where he interviews country stars and runs music videos. The show runs almost 4 years. In October, once again, KNIX is named Station of the Year by the CMA Country Music Association.

John Michaels
Interviews Reba
McEntire on
Steppin Out
(courtesy of Chris
Braden)

I was over an hour late to my interview with Larry Daniels for a part time opening. I got lost trying to find the station. I finally stopped at a pay phone (before cellphones) and called. "John, what happened to you?" Larry said. I apologized profusely and realized I was on Gilbert road in GILBERT, not GILBERT DRIVE in Tempe, the dirt road that lead to the station! Larry laughed and told me I wasn't even in the right town! But he hired me on to start the following Sunday morning. Larry taught me how to work a crowd. He said; What sets KNIX apart from other stations is we make the listeners feel special. Go out there and fight for every listener."

John Michaels, Air Talent (1981-1997)

Top to bottom: STEPPIN OUT TV show with John Michaels and singer Travis Tritt, 1990's (courtesy of Keith Ritchie)

Another shot of Travis Tritt on the STEPPIN OUT TV show (courtesy of Keith Ritchie)

John Michaels STEPPIN OUT TV show at the Coliseum with concertgoers (courtesy of Keith Ritchie)

I had the privilege to be a part of the KNIX family for over 4 years as KPNX TV 12 partnered with the station on a country video show called STEPPIN OUT! KNIX had clout and major connections in the country music community giving viewers premiere access to the country stars up close and personal. We had great support from Buddy and Michael Owens and guidance from Sandy Lovejoy, editor of the KNIX magazine. Standards were high. The degree of professionalism and caring was not lost on me. I'm thankful for the experience.

Keith Ritchie, Producer / Director 'KNIX Steppin Out' (1991-1994)

Top left: Buck Owens, Marilyn and Larry Daniels on Larry's 20th Anniversary at KNIX (courtesy of Michael Owens)

Top right: Buddy Owens and Merle Haggard (courtesy of Larry Daniels)

Right: Larry Daniels and Michael Owens manning the KNIX store at Arizona State Fair, 1990's (courtesy of Vicki Fiorelli-Starkovich)

1992

W. Steven Martin

*K*NIX MAKES RATINGS HISTORY WITH THE HIGHEST TOTAL OF LISTENERS ever with 443,600 listeners. This is 100,000 more than the number two station. The station partners with the city of Phoenix and NewsChannel 3 for the FABULOUS PHOENIX FOURTH OF JULY, headliners include Dwight Yoakam, Little Texas and others. In September MORNING MAN W. Steven Martin is named Large Market Air Personality of the year by the CMA.

Top: W. Steven Martin, winner of TWO CMA CRYSTAL AWARDS, also continues his community involvement with the 911 Police Toy Drive Program he founded in 1985 that has now given over six million gifts to children! (picture courtesy of WSM Promotions)

Bottom: Dwight Yoakam in Concert, KNIX Fabulous Phoenix 4th of July show, 1992 (courtesy of Michael Owens)

Opposite page top left: Dwight Yoakam, Buddy Owens, Buck Owens and Michael Owens, 1992 (courtesy of Michael Owens)

Bottom left: Phoenix Open Pro-Am Golf Tournament, L to R; Michael Owens, Karston Solheim, PING Golf Clubs, Vince Gill, Buck Owens, Buddy Owens, Mel Owens Jr, and Glen Campbell, 1992 (courtesy of Chris Braden)

Right: W Steven Martin "showered with honors" (courtesy of Larry Daniels)

My husband and I used to go to the KNIX nights around town. We knew all the on-air personalities. Danced at Mr. Lucky's, went to all the sponsored concerts at Graham Central Station and Toolie's Country. George Strait showed up with no cowboy hat one night, no one recognized him! Fun to see Garth before he was a big star. We were dedicated KNIX listeners.

Pawnee Erin Carter Long time KNIX listener, nearly 30 years

TOWN CRIER

Lynn Dalbey

Radio host showered with honors

Chandler resident W. Steven Martin, host of the Valley's No. 1 morning radio show, has received another award to add to his more than 2,000 plaques and certificates of appreciation for service to Arizona communities.

Gov. Rose Mofford presented Martin with The Country Music Foundation Award of Appreciation for dedicated service to country music and generous support of his home state and its citizens.

"W. Steven has continually given to our community in many different ways," Mofford said. "He is one of the most popular radio personalities in Arizona and a true professional who brings fun and goodwill wherever he appears."

Martin has been broadcasting in Phoenix for more than 20 years. He is best known for his morning show *Shower Song* on KNIX (102.5 FM). His show has been broadcast by satellite, and he has been recognized nationally as *Billboard* magazine's Personality of the Year and has been a finalist three times for the Country Music Association's Radio Personality of the Year.

Martin and his Arizona Charity Riders have spent a great deal of their personal time riding throughout the state collecting toys for various Christmas programs for the needy and the homeless. They have worked for the American Cancer Society, Arizona Easter Seal Society and many other local and statewide charities.

He has been a member of the Maricopa County Sheriff's Jeep Posse and Search and Rescue Unit for seven years.

I have seen Martin and his Charity Riders' generosity at work. Congratulations for a well-deserved award.

1993

$\mathcal{I}$N APRIL, THE STATION IS ONCE AGAIN NAMED COUNTRY STATION OF THE YEAR by the California based ACM, Academy of Country Music on NBC TV. By mid-year 1993, KNIX can claim ratings dominance for 43 of the last 45 ratings surveys dating back 13 years. KNIX is featured in national trade magazine R & R, Radio and Records and local Phoenix Gazette for KNIX 25th Anniversary. At years end, the station sponsors the 10th Annual Tempe Fiesta Bowl block party with nearly 150,000 attending.

My most memorable KNIX story concerns GM Michael Owens. My assistant engineer Dave Sanford and I worked almost 20 hours straight one weekend to replace a main studio audio console. It had to be on the air Monday morning. After working tirelessly that long weekend, I came in early Monday to make sure everything was ready for the morning show team. I ran into Michael in the hallway. He stopped me, put his hands on my shoulders and said; "Now John, don't forget to take some time off for working so hard this weekend." Being shocked I said to Michael, "You're not a real GM are you!?" We both laughed. It was a great place to work.

John P. Baker, Chief Engineer (1997-1998)

Michael Owens accepts Academy of Country Music award for station of the year, 1993 (courtesy of Michael Owens)

Steve Goddard hangs out with rocker Alice Cooper at a KNIX Celebrity Golf tournament (courtesy of Steve Goddard)

My 13 years at KNIX (6 under the ownership of the Owens family), gives me a unique perspective to compare the station during and after the "Buck" years. Simply put, during the red, white and blue guitar years there was a great sense of pride to be working at one of the greatest radio stations in the entire country. Everything was first class!

The facilities (spotlessly maintained), included a separate weight facility with a full time trainer, yoga classes, a half basketball court, KNIX magazine, and KNIX merchandise that included shirts, jackets, caps, pewter key chains, even KNIX baby shirts!

Maybe someday I'll put enough stories together to fill a few pages, but this is Jim's book (thank god) and I would like to share one story in particular-

I met so many artists local and national and still have so many wonderful friends from my 13 years as the KNIX afternoon drive personality, but my biggest story may be the miracle of how I was hired by Larry Daniels.

In November 1992 I should have robbed a bank.

I was off the air, out of work, and no one would give me an opportunity. When I dropped by to see Larry about working at KNIX, he told me he's just hired someone for the afternoon drive shift that came from another country radio station. He had just been burned by the morning team of Hawke and Hunter who had come from a rock station and vowed he wouldn't hire another person that didn't have country radio experience. (Never mind I was born in Muskogee, Oklahoma, and was raised in a small town 20 miles away-Yes, I am an Okie from Muskogee)

Flash forward to 1993. I was a week away from a McDonalds job application when I got an idea. The only way Larry would know how I would sound on KNIX would be to fabricate a recording of me on KNIX with the music, jingles, and personality to fit the station – which wasn't hard.

I recorded a couple hours of KNIX off the radio, broke down the format, lifted their jingles from the recording, and sat down to make a fake tape to give to Larry-which I did that same week. A day later I got a call from Larry that he's listened to the tape and wanted me to come in to talk.

I don't have a fulltime shift for you. The only thing I have open is a Saturday morning shift from 6-10 am. But I'll give you all the vacation fill in work for the entire summer.

I took it, and by August they let the fellow they'd hired the previous November go, and hired me full time.

I'm eternally grateful for that life changing opportunity, and I thank Larry and the Owens family every time I see them. I met so many country stars I grew up with and loved (Stonewall Jackson and Merle Haggard were my favorites) and so many people continue to be close friends to this day, especially W. Steven Martin.

.....And I thank all of you who ever listened.... I love you all.

Steve Goddard (1993-2005)

Above: Steve Goddard with Buck Owens autographed Red, White and Blue Fender Telecaster guitar (courtesy of Steve Goddard)

Left: One of the customized "country star" KNIX bumper stickers featuring George Strait

1994

IN FEBRUARY, THE STATION WELCOMES new morning team, HAWK and HUNTER. In March the station announces the formation of John Michaels and Bobby Lewis as the new afternoon "team." Nearly a year later they become the new morning show team on a speculative basis with the departure of HAWK and HUNTER. Shortly after, Carolyn Coffey joins the morning mix and the show becomes, "JOHN, BOBBY and COFFEY" in the morning. The station co-sponsors another Fabulous Phoenix 4th of July concert. Trisha Yearwood and Clay Walker headline. In September, KNIX brings on the syndicated BLAIR GARNER-AFTER MIDNIGHT programming.

> *I was in radio for over 20 years and working at KNIX was the best radio job I ever had. Worked with fantastic people like Michael and Buddy Owens and Larry Daniels. Larry, he was the one who hired me and I'm pretty sure he might have regretted it?!*

John Michaels and I became the first afternoon country radio on-air team in the USA to my knowledge. Then we spent time in morning drive as John, Bobby and Coffee along with Carolyn Coffey. I also happily assisted John Michaels doing music, new's and notes on the "STEPPIN OUT" TV show on Channel 12 on Saturday nights. Great memories.

Bobby Lewis (1989- 1997)

Buddy Owens, Bob Podolsky, Garth Brooks, Michael Owens and Larry Daniels, 1990's. "It's a Penguin Party". (courtesy of Vicki Florelli-Starkovich)

When you find yourself in the right place at the right time, then you're pretty lucky. Working for the best country radio station in the U.S. was unforgettable. One day, PD Larry Daniels stopped by my sales desk. He introduced me to a young man who took off his hat when he shook my hand. He said he was excited to have his songs played on KNIX. I wished him good luck. It was Garth Brooks! Another time Glen Campbell sang "By the time I get to Phoenix" a cappela just to me at the first KNIX Celebrity Golf Tournament. Doesn't get any better than that.

Patty Kincaid, KNIX sales (1982-1999)

Top left: Bobby Lewis, Carolyn Coffey and John Michaels, KNIX mornings, late 90's (courtesy of Chris Braden)

Top right: KNIX FUN VAN, 1990'S (courtesy of Larry Daniels)

Above: Larry Daniels, Singer Clint Black, John Conlee and Bill Bachand, owner of TOOLIES COUNTRY nightclub, Phoenix, 1990's (courtesy of Chris Braden)

1995

$\mathcal{I}$N JUNE, THE STATION DROPS THE SYNDICATED "AFTER MIDNIGHT" SHOW in response to Larry Daniels research showing listeners desire to hear their "All time favorites" not fulfilled by the satellite show. In July, the station again stages another FABULOUS PHOENIX FOURTH of July concert featuring Patty Loveless and Diamond Rio on the KNIX stage.

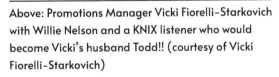

Above: Promotions Manager Vicki Fiorelli-Starkovich with Willie Nelson and a KNIX listener who would become Vicki's husband Todd!! (courtesy of Vicki Fiorelli-Starkovich)

Top right: The day diet guru RICHARD SIMMONS came to town with the KNIX promotional staff (courtesy of Vicki Fiorelli-Starkovich)

Right: Channel 12 sports director Bill Denny did sports on KNIX in the 90's (courtesy of Larry Daniels)

1996

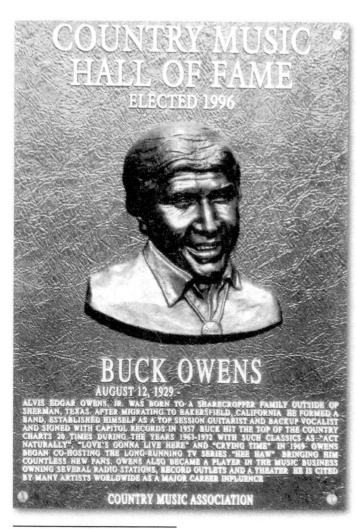

Buck Owens in the Country Music
Hall of Fame, Nashville (courtesy of
Michael Owens)

COUNTRY SPIRIT MAGAZINE BECOMES KNIX MAGAZINE with re-designed cover and new format. 100,000 copies are printed each month. In July, the KNIX FABULOUS PHOENIX FOURTH of July features The Mavericks and Junior Brown. Huge crowds attend. Station starts KNIX CONNECTION, a telephone computer dating service. BILLBOARD MAGAZINE names KNIX Major Market Station of The Year. Larry Daniels named Program Director and Buddy Owens named music director of the year.

Buck Owens is inducted into the COUNTRY MUSIC HALL of FAME in Nashville and honored on the nationally televised CMA awards. Later that year, Buck is inducted into the Nashville Songwriters HOF. Steve Harmon and Carrie Wilson are named new morning team in 1996. In December, LeAnn Rimes headlines the annual Fiesta Bowl New Years Eve Block party. It's now a Fiesta Bowl event.

Michael and Buddy Owens admire their dad's Country Music Hall of Fame plaque in Nashville (courtesy of Michael Owens)

For years while at KPLX, Dallas I watched what was nicknamed "The Phoenix Mafia." Grateful Larry Daniels hired me. Wonderful, smart people in every position of the building. Massive amounts of "what can we do to help you win?" And we did ---over and over. George King, Steve Goddard, W. Steven Martin, Buddy Owens, Michael Owens...Hall of Fame management, personalities all day and night. When I tell people about Vicki Fiorelli's promotion team featuring a KNIX Hot Air Balloon...minds blown. There is no doubt those call letters on my resume helped me my entire career.

Steve Harmon, Steve & Carrie Mornings (1996-1997)
Country Radio Hall of Fame Nashville

W. Steven Martin and the station won many Music Industry Awards (courtesy of WSM promotions)

STEVE & CARRIE
AND
THE MORNING
CREW

Early Mornings
5:30am-10am

Pictured left to right: Steve Ludwig-Traffic,
Marty McNeil-News, Steve Harmon,
Dave Burns-Sports, and Carrie Wilson.

GEORGE KING	W. STEVEN MARTIN	STEVE GODDARD	TOMMY C.	JASON CHRISTOPHER
Midmornings	Middays	Afternoons	Evenings	Overnights
10am-Noon	Noon-3pm	3-7pm	7pm-Midnight	Midnight-5:30am

KNIX's success had a lot to do with two things. First, the wonderful team of people we had working with us, as they were all just brilliant. And second, the people who created, managed and promoted the music and their willingness to work with us so well.

The station started its rise to fame when my brother Michael and program director Larry Daniels began working together. As the role of music director evolved it gave me the space to create and nuture relationships with the artists, managers, record promoters, and our listeners that brought endless benefits. We rolled out the red carpet when artists like George, Reba, Alabama, Garth Brooks and many others came to visit us with an experience they would not forget. Larry always said; "You never know when the next big star will come knocking." Many of these stars "endorsements" in television commercials told KNIX listeners that we were "one of the best country stations in the USA."

We were very proud to be selected to win the ACM or CMA Country radio station of the Year award, several times! Going to work each day was so much fun. Everyone worked hard through the years. From the on-air-personalities to the sales executives to our research department and the entire support staff. Many talented people came through our doors and later would go on to bigger and better careers in radio and the music business.

My brother Michael was the best radio manager I've ever known. He knew how to give someone a task and then the room and motivation to get it done. Larry Daniels our program director, had the "knack" for knowing what listeners wanted. No wonder they are both in the COUNTRY RADIO HALL OF FAME. Bob Podolsky, our General sales manager put together a wonderful team and he never sacrificed the "sound" just to make a few extra dollars.

Finally, our promotions department was "top shelf" with fun events, bumper stickers, concerts and KNIX nights at the local clubs. The late Sandy Lovejoy was such an asset with meticulous writing skills. No one could interview an artist like Sandy. So many names through the years. I love em all.

Buddy Alan Owens, Music Director (1986-1999)

Opposite page: KNIX airstaff and morning show, late 1990's (courtesy of Steve Harmon)

Top: Buddy Alan Owens charted several national country hits in the seventies, toured with Buck Owens and also appeared on the TV show HEE HAW. (courtesy of Buddy Owens)

Above: Steve Harmon, Vicki Fiorelli-Starkovich, baseball's Tommy LaSorda and Carrie Wilson (courtesy of Steve Harmon)

1997

*T*HE GROUP ALABAMA HEADLINES THE FABULOUS PHOENIX FOURTH OF JULY concert in downtown Phoenix. The Real Country Network has grown to be one of the largest satellite networks in less than 8 years reaching over 1.2 million listeners weekly on 150 affiliates. In 1997, Michael Owens, CEO of Owens Broadcasting and Delbert Lewis, President of MAC America Communications, announce the formation of OwensMAC Radio, LLC. The era of radio consolidation will bring KESZ radio (KEZ) and KNIX under one umbrella to better compete in the marketplace.

KNIX is once again the most listened to station in Phoenix. Ratings show a 7.0 share of 12 plus audience. Times were changing in the radio industry. The market is being carved up in smaller pieces. A decade earlier KNIX was on top with a 15.3 share! In September 1997, former jazz station KOAZ-FM becomes "Wild Country" with Tim and Willy in the morning, formerly of competitor KMLE. In October 97, KNIX Magazine publishes its 10th Anniversary issue.

Left: The group ALABAMA became RCA records "Artists of the decade" 1990's. Top row L to R: RCA record executives, members of ALABAMA; Front row, RCA's Carson Schreiber, Buddy and Michael Owens and Larry Daniels (courtesy of Michael Owens). Right: George King and LeAnn Rimes perusing a KNIX magazine, 1990's (courtesy of George King)

Who would have thought that there was a time when advertisers did not want to buy the country music format? They didn't believe it would get them the results they were looking for. But great leadership and vision convinced the market it was a smart choice. Fast forward through Urban Cowboy, Alan Jackson, Reba, George Strait and Garth Brooks, and the rest is history. I was fortunate to be a part of the most prestigious, well respected and successful radio station in America! The management staff created the blueprint that others followed. Winner of the first Marconi radio award and countless ACM and CMA awards. KNIX was the best radio station ever!

Shanna McCoy, Sales Dept (1982-1999)

Top: Steve Goddard hanging out with Superstar Toby Keith (courtesy of Steve Goddard)

Above: Brian White, Glen Campbell & Steve Goddard warble a tune! (courtesy of Steve Goddard)

1998

*I*N JUNE, LARRY DANIELS AND BUDDY OWENS ARE NAMED RADIO & RECORDS trade magazine Country Program and Music Director of the year at the R & R convention. Local research shows the market cannot support a third major country station. Michael Owens pulls the plug on WILD COUNTRY and moves Tim and Willy to the morning show on KNIX effective June 15th. In August 1998, the station again captures three major BILLBOARD and AIRPLAY MONITOR country radio awards, voted on by readership. KNIX named station of the year, Larry Daniels wins Program Director of the year, and Buddy Owens again named Music Director of the year for the eighth time in the last decade.

Tim and Willie welcome country legend WAYLON JENNINGS to the morning show, late 90's (courtesy of Tim Hattrick)

Opposite page top: House of Broadcasting Michael Owens "Roast" invite 1998. Middle: Michael Owens gets "roasted" at House of Broadcasting event with Tim and Willie. Bottom: Buddy, Bonnie, Buck and Michael Owens at HOBI "ROAST" 1998 (all three pictures courtesy of Mary Morrison)

Before Michael Owens came to Arizona, KNIX was regarded as a little "obscure" station. But his policies, upbeat attitude, hard work and charisma made KNIX the premiere station. The many years Michael was GM and Buddy the music director, the buzz was on KNIX. It didn't hurt, in the process, that Michael met and married Kristin. When House of Broadcasting decided to start a Celebrity Toast in 1998 we had many media personality choices but unanimously decided Michael deserved the honor!

Mary Morrison, President, House of Broadcasting / Former Media buyer

During one sweltering summer week in 1984, I helped my brother build a patio cover on my folk's house in Scottsdale. He controlled the radio and loved KNIX. Every day, it was nothing but Dolly, Eddie Rabbitt, George Strait, The Judds and Julio and Willie. I swear I heard Tom T. Hall sing "I love little baby ducks" at least 15 times. It was not cool and I was NOT country, NOT yet.

Thirteen years later, I'm listening to my answering machine over and over—I couldn't believe it, "Tim, its BUCK OWENS---I just want to welcome you and Willy to the KNIX family! You guys are going to be great and have so much fun." Wow!

Watching HEE HAW with my dad all those years ago, if you had told me one of the characters from "cornfield county" had left a message I'd have wondered; "what's an answering machine?" Seriously, one of the great blessings of my life was to work for Buck Owens at KNIX alongside Michael, Buddy and the entire Owens family. They were kind, generous and classy and Buck was right—we did have FUN!

Tim Hattrick, Tim & Willy Morning show (1997-1999)

In April 1997, Tim Hattrick and I were working in Chicago when we found out the station changed format and we were out. The next day Michael Owens called and offered us a gig. I get home one night and my wife says; "you'll never guess who called today."? Who, I asked? "Buck Owens calling to welcome you to the station." It was truly an honor to work for Michael, Buddy, Bob and Larry. They had class and respect from the country music industry. Great working with pro's in every department including great on-air personalities. Did I mention KNIX had a gym and basketball court? Boy, do I miss those days.

William Carmichael (Willy D. Loon), Tim and Willy morning show (1997-1999)

Above: Michael and Kristin Owens, 1992 (courtesy of Mary Morrison)

Left: Big Stars were always stopping by the station. Here is Wynonna Judd visiting with Vicki Fiorelli-Starkovich and George King (courtesy of Vicki Fiorelli-Starkovich)

1999

$\mathcal{W}$EDNESDAY MARCH 17TH, 1999 MICHAEL OWENS, VP, GM OF KNIX ANNOUNCES in an emotional meeting to his staff, that after nearly 31 years the station would be sold, along with KEZ in a separate transaction to JACOR COMMUNICATIONS. (which would later become Clear Channel and now iHeart Media) KNIX sold for a record breaking $84 million dollars. "It's bittersweet, Michael Owens was quoted in the Arizona Republic newspaper. "My dream was to keep these stations and buy more, but that wasn't going to happen." It was the end of an era. Owens said the decision to sell became clear when the Phoenix radio market had changed since the nationwide Telecom bill was enacted by Congress in 1996 therefore deregulating several communications industries including radio. The company essentially would have had to purchase more stations to be competitive.

KNIX-FM CONTINUES TODAY AS ONE OF THE TOP COUNTRY STATIONS IN AMERICA!

CRS Nashville, L to R: Buddy Owens, Lon Helton, Country Aircheck, singer Paul Overstreet, Bob Podolsky and Michael Owens (courtesy of Lon Helton)

Top left: Veteran KNIX sales account executives, Leyla Kirdar-Haupert, Michael Owens, Shanna McCoy, Patty Kincaid, Buddy Owens and Bob Podolsky, 2018 (courtesy of Leyla Kirdar-Haupert)

Left: Sales folks John Browning, Leslie Schaffer, Leyla Kirdar-Haupert, Art Morales and L.J. Waggoner (courtesy of Leyla Kirdar-Haupert)

Above: Jim West and Buddy Alan Owens, Phoenix, 2019

The KNIX Research department was founded in 1980. I was the first research director for the company. Michael and Larry hired me while I was attending ASU. KNIX was a pioneer and on the cutting edge of in-house audience research. It was quite an investment.

We had a mini call-center at the station. Every evening, using a phone book, our team would randomly call people asking what radio station they listened to. When we identified country music listeners, we'd play hooks of songs over the phone to them and ask their opinion (was it familiar, a favorite, just ok, tired of it etc.) We played the hooks off a cassette recorder wired into the phones in those days.

It took hours to prepare the reports each week until we advanced to computers. Our first computer was a NorthStar Advantage (pre-IBM pc) Simultaneously we developed our own custom software for tabulating and analyzing the data. Each week we provided programming and management a comprehensive report of all the radio stations in Phoenix, a detailed demographic report that showed what songs were trending up and down and comments from listeners.

KNIX also worked with research companies to conduct on-going audience studies and listener focus groups. Continuous research gave KNIX a unique advantage when it came to charting their course and maintaining unprecedented ratings dominance through the years.

Michael Mallace, Research Director (1980-1984)

Mike Owens and Staff, 1998

Parting Shots!

Top left: Jim West in the eighties with a young Crystal Gayle (courtesy of Jim West). Top Right and above: Bill Heywood, a very popular Phoenix air personality, had the number one morning show for years at KOY radio, an Adult contemporary station. On April Fools' Day 1986 Bill Heywood and W. Steven Martin, the KNIX morning man traded places and claimed they were the other! No listeners were FOOLED but played along and enjoyed the day (courtesy of Larry Daniels)

Oppisite Page. Top left: "Human KNIX guitars" L to R Tim Hattrick, Alan Sledge and Willie DeLoon, 1990's Doing anything for attention (courtesy of Larry Daniels). Top right: Another KNIX event in Phoenix, L to R: Bobby Lewis, R.J. Curtis, W. Steven Martin, GM Michael Owens and John Michaels (courtesy of R.J. Curtis). Top middle right: The "G" man came to town in the 1990's, Garth Brooks flanked by R. J. Curtis on the left and Buddy Alan Owens on the right. Bottom: T-shirt Model promoting, stylin' and marketing a KNIX T-Shirt (courtesy of Larry Daniels)

In Memoriam

Buck Owens, Station Owner 1968-1999

Sandy Lovejoy, KNIX Magazine Writer/ Editor

Doug Baker, Air Talent

Bill Kramer, Air Talent

John Buchanan, Air Talent

Bobby Butler, Air Talent

Jason Christopher, Air Talent

Mike Patrick---Air Talent

Bill Denny, Channel 12 TV and KNIX Sports

Sandy Elder, Sales Assistant

Bennett Freeman, Sales

Mark Kopelman, Sales

Geoff Erb, Production

Dave Crosier, Air Talent

Dwight Yoakam, Sandy and Buck Owens

Sandy's last issue of KNIX Magazine, June/July 1999

In Loving Memory of

Sandy Lovejoy

1946-2000

The country music industry, broadcasters and KNIX listeners were saddened by the loss of a great friend, Sandy Lovejoy. Sandy succumbed to breast cancer in February, 2000.

Sandy was loved by everyone in the country music industry as well as her KNIX colleagues and KNIX fans. Sandy began her career at KNIX Radio in early 1987 as editor of the KNIX/Tune In Magazine. In 1989, under the leadership of Sandy the magazine went solo , dropped its affiliation with Tune In and KNIX/Country Spirit Magazine was born. Along with her duties of editor of the KNIX Magazine, Sandy wrote for many country music artists as well as local Phoenix newspapers, writing under the name of The Phantom Honky Tonkers.

Sandy loved country music and the people associated with it. She was a respected writer and a great friend to country music artists, management, record companies, and everyone connected with the industry. Sandy Lovejoy will be missed by everyone at KNIX and all her friends in country music!

With Mark Wills

With Billy Dean at the KNIX studio

With her dear friends Wynonna and Naomi Judd

With Chris LeDoux and the KNIX gang!

KNIX
FM 102-5

"The kind of people I enjoy being around are people who are upbeat, enthusiastic and positive. Sandy Lovejoy was definitely one of those people. I don't recall a time that she wasn't a pure pleasure and a lot of fun to be around. I was always so tickled to be called her friend. And there was no doubt in anyone's mind that she loved country music. I know I speak for a lot of people when I say country music lost a good one but God got one of the best."

– Reba McEntire, May 11, 2000

About the Author

JIM WEST

*J*IM WEST BEGAN HIS BROADCASTING CAREER IN THE EARLY 70'S working part-time while serving in the U.S. Air Force. By the end of the decade, he would be working for Buck Owens and the Owens family at KNIX in Phoenix, Arizona. Over the next 40 plus years, the experience and skills he learned at KNIX served him well in radio stations in cities like Indianapolis, Albuquerque, Baltimore and Tucson. He worked as an on-air radio personality as well as in programming and management positions in radio, television and satellite radio operations.

West is a two-time finalist for Nashville's Country Radio Hall of Fame and a finalist for Large Market Country Music Association (CMA) Broadcast Personality of the Year. He served on the Academy of Country Music (ACM) Board of Directors and was inducted into the Greater Arizona Country Music Hall of Fame in 2019.

In retirement, West has become a music historian and author. His first book was *THE PHOENIX SOUND, A History of Twang and Rockabilly Music in Arizona*. He is also a co-writer on the book *RAY ODOM; A Lifetime of Radio, Records and Racehorses*.

He continues to write for major magazines and can be heard on Satellite and Internet radio stations in many areas of the country.

Additional book by author: ***The Phoenix Sound: A History of Twang and Rockabilly Music in Arizona*** available on Amazon and Barnes and Noble.

The largest Billboard in the state of
Arizona advertising KNIX was seen by
thousands of people every year along
Interstate 17 in Phoenix

CPSIA information can be obtained
at www.ICGtesting.com
Printed in the USA
LVHW011425080622
720763LV00011B/715